The Inner Naturalist Journal

Summer & Early Fall
JULY – SEPTEMBER

ABUNDANCE & TRANSITION

developed by **Lari Jo Wallace Edwards**

Copyright © 2025 Lari Jo Wallace Edwards

ISBN: 979-8-9990023-1-0

All rights reserved. No part of this book may be reproduced or transmitted in any form or by any means, electronic or mechanical, including photocopying, recording or by any information storage and retrieval system without written permission of the publisher, except for the inclusion of brief quotations in a review.

INTRODUCTION

Hi, I'm Lari Jo — a Nature Connected Transformational Coach, lifelong lover of the outdoors, and someone who found her way back to wholeness by following the quiet, powerful rhythms of the Earth.

I haven't always known how to live in alignment with the seasons. For years, I moved through life on overdrive — giving, striving, achieving — until my body, heart, and spirit demanded I slow down. Like many of you, I've walked through grief, burnout, and major life transitions. Nature didn't just hold me through those times — it offered a new way forward.

What I've discovered, and now teach, is that we are not separate from the seasons — we are the seasons. We cycle through growth and rest, expansion and release. And when we begin to honor these natural shifts, we return to a wiser, more grounded version of ourselves.

This journal — covering July through September — is your invitation to experience the fullness of Summer & Early Fall as a season of abundance and transition.

This is a time of connection, gratitude, and preparation. The days are still long, the sun still warm, but there's a subtle shift if you pause to notice. Maybe it's in the gold of the morning light, the first fallen leaf, or your own body's desire to slow down after a season of high energy.

Inside this journal, you'll find seasonal prompts, reflection practices, and simple rituals to help you align more deeply with this powerful turning point on the Wheel of the Year. Whether it's journaling during sunset, walking slowly through a field of tall grass, or gathering with friends under the stars, each practice is here to help you stay connected — to nature, to your truth, and to the fullness of this season.

This is a season of harvesting and simplifying, of deepening relationships and savoring the present moment. It's a time to ask:

- What am I proud of?
- Where do I feel most abundant?
- What am I preparing to let go of as the light begins to shift?

Through my coaching work with Inner-NATURALIST, I help individuals reconnect to their inner landscapes through nature connection tools like sit spots, neurographic drawing, story-sharing, and seasonal reflection. You are never alone on this journey, and there is no rush. Nature never hurries, and yet everything gets done.

You don't have to push to bloom — you're already in full flower.

Let this journal be your companion as you soak in the sweetness of summer and begin to prepare — gently, intentionally — for what's next.

With a grateful heart and an open path ahead, *Happy Nature Connecting!*

—*Lari Jo*

The Wheel of the Year

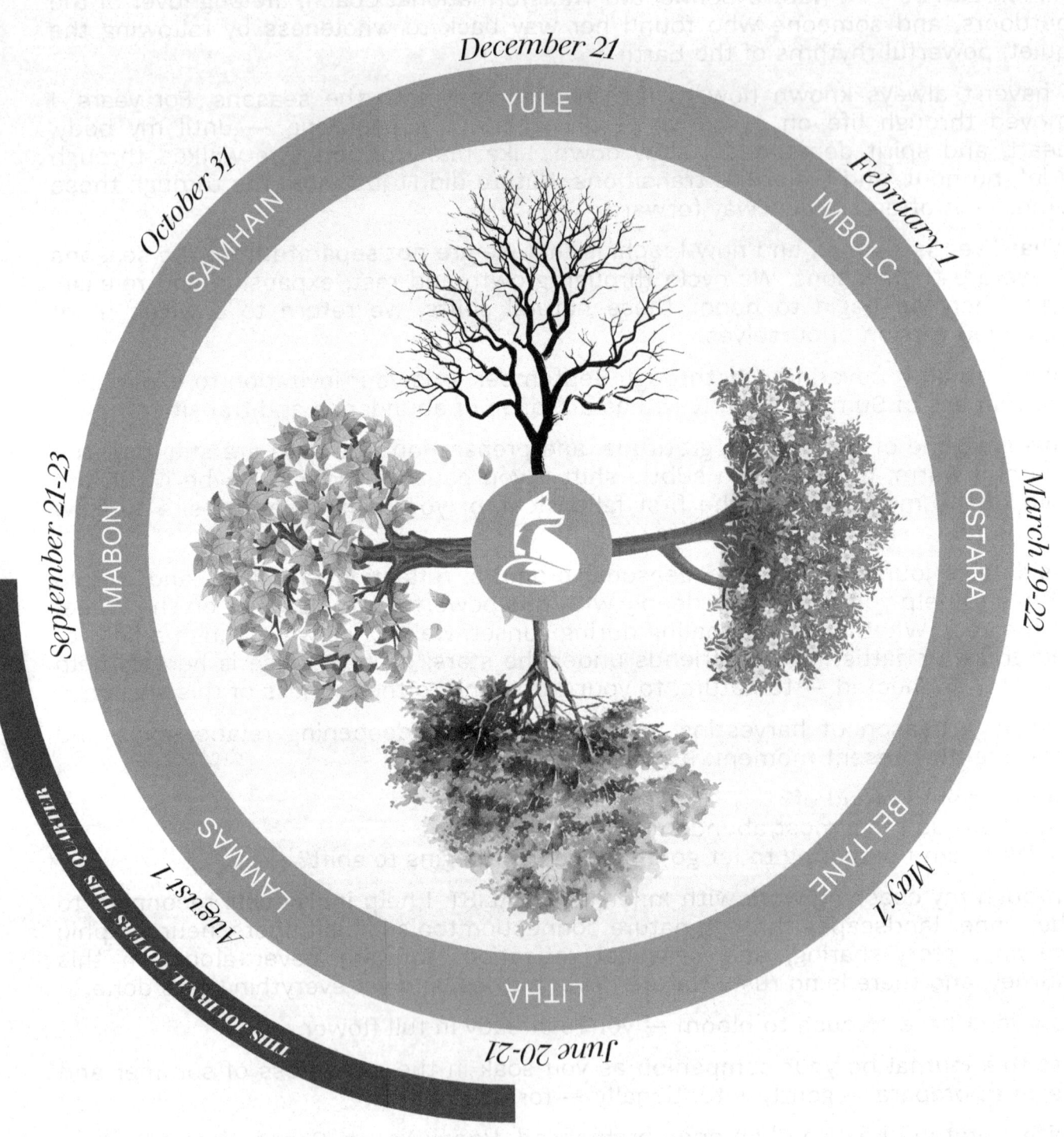

The Wheel of the Year

Living these cycles helps you to love and respect nature, and live in harmony with the earth. One of the main beliefs is "Harm None." This includes animals, humans, and nature.

1 SAMAHAIN
Moving Towards Winter

Samhain is the celebration that is the origin the final harvest. It is a time of deep work. Slow down and honor the past and any Death that has occurred while embracing the dark season of the year. Take time to reflect on the past year and set intentions for the upcoming year that starts with Yule.

2 YULE
Winter Solstice

Yule celebrates rebirth and renewal. This is because the shortest day and longest night occur on the solstice. After the solstice, the days start to get longer, and Yule celebrates the beginning of the return of the sun. With shorter days, we may need more rest and experience less energy. For many of us, our inclination is to withdraw indoors in Winter, but you can still (and should) enjoy nature in the winter. Celebrate with story telling, Set goals for they new longer productive days ahead, feast with family and friends, Spend time giving back to nature.

3 IMBOLC
Moving Towards Spring

The celebration of Imbolc is a celebration of fire and light. It symbolizes the halfway point between the winter solstice (Yule) and the spring equinox (Ostara). The word "imbolc" means "in the belly of the Mother," because the seeds of spring are beginning to stir in the belly of Mother Earth. Around this time of year, many herd animals give birth to their first offspring of the year, or are heavily pregnant. This creation of life's milk is a part of the symbolic hope for spring. This is a time when shoots begin to sprout, buds begin to peon and light and warmth are beginning to touch our days. Celebrate with Inspiration and time in nature, set your wellness goals, and plant seeds literally and figuratively.

4 OSTARA
Spring Equinox

Ostara represents spring and new beginnings. Ostara symbolizes fertility, rebirth, and renewal. This time of year marked the beginning of the agricultural cycle, and farmers would start planting seeds. Ostara is a day of perfect balance when the sun can be seen directly above the earth's equator. It is the time when light and dark are completely equal. One might go outside to meditate and perform a simple ritual to welcome the spring, go outside, color eggs, tend to your spring garden, and feast with family.

5 BELTANE
Moving Towards Summer

Beltane falls about halfway between the spring equinox (Ostara) and the coming summer solstice, (Litha). The holiday celebrates spring as its peak, and the coming summer. his holiday is associated very strongly with fertility, lust, power and abundance. Decorate with fresh flowers, take action on projects, enjoy abundance, love, and passion. This is a time of dancing, fairies, and fun! Enjoy it!

★ 6 LITHA
Summer Solstice

Litha occurs on the summer solstice, and celebrates the beginning of summer. It celebrates the sun's power and the longest day of the year. Celebrate by connecting with nature on a deeper level; walks in a forest or natural location, walking barefoot (grounding) either in your backyard or on a beach can help you feel connected to the earth as can sitting by a bonfire, meditating outside, or just gardening.

★ 7 LAMMAS
Autumn

Lammas, which is about halfway between the summer solstice (Litha) and the fall equinox (Mabon). It celebrates the first harvest or grain harvest. Celebrate by baking bread, giving thanks, reflect on everything you have created this year, make a cornhusk doll or collect seeds for the next year.

★ 8 MABON
Autumn Equinox

Mabon celebrates the autumnal equinox. It celebrates the second harvest which includes berries. It is a time of balance the days and nights are once again equal. As the harvest completes, the leaves begin to change color and the warmth of summer is replaced by pleasant, breezy days. This is a time to reap the bounty of summer, to plant new seeds for the spring, to contemplate new ideas, and to make medicine. Celebrate with introspection and grace, set intentions that involve decrease and reduction such as ending bad relationships, unhealthy habits or self destructive beliefs, write down your blessings from the past year, have a picnic in nature and decorate your porch for fall.

The Wheel of the Year
Intention Setting

LITHA
Summer Solstice

How will I connect to nature this season?

What actions will I take?

How will I enjoy abundance? Love? Passion?

LAMMAS
Autumn

How will I connect to nature this season?

What actions will I take?

How will I enjoy abundance? Love? Passion?

MABON
Autumn Equinox

How will I connect to nature this season?

What actions will I take?

How will I enjoy abundance? Love? Passion?

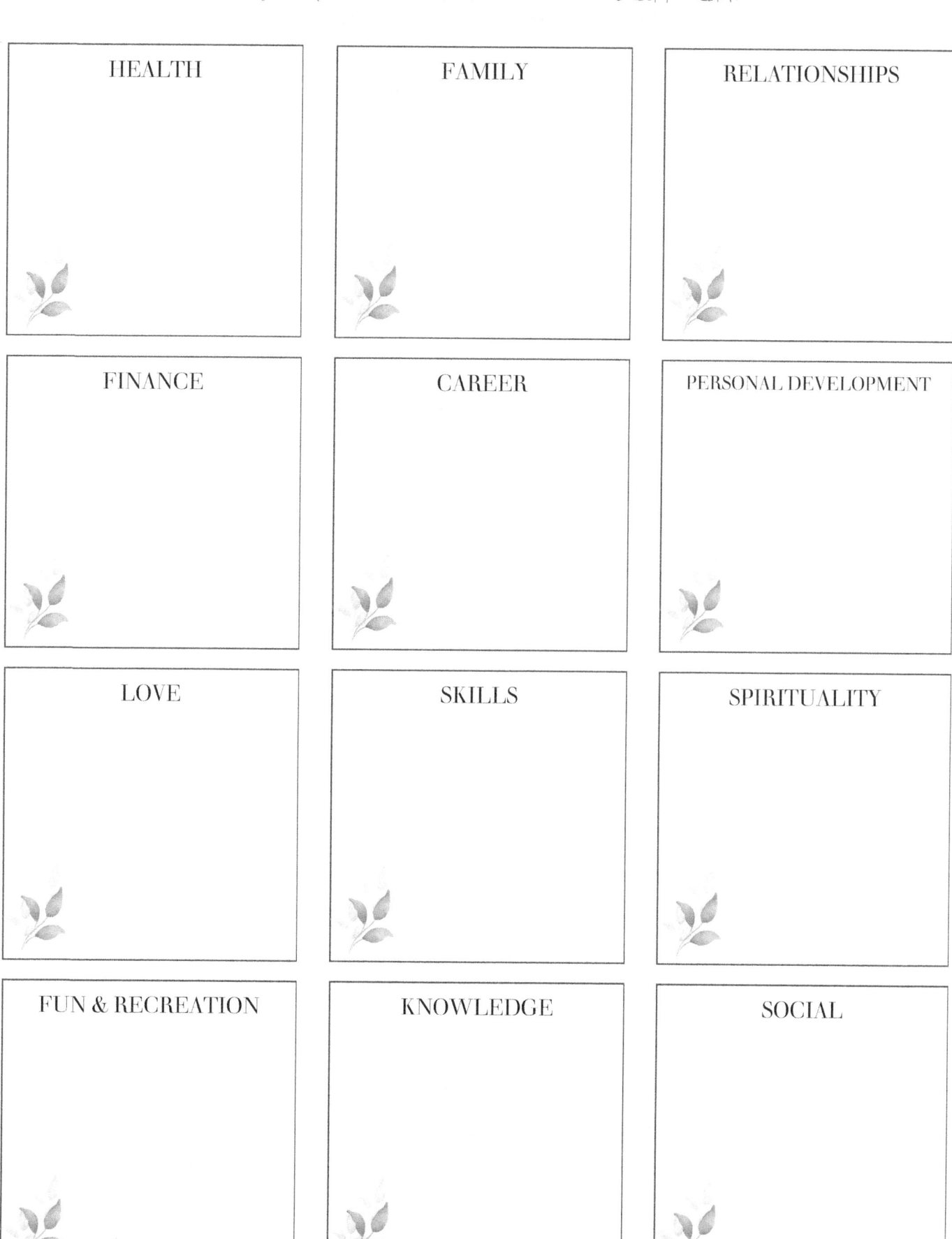

Summer & Early Fall
Season Goals

Align your personal growth with nature's rhythms.

MESSAGE TO MYSELF THIS SEASON

THIS SEASON'S TOP 3 GOALS

1.

2.

3.

TO DO THIS SEASON

- [ ]
- [ ]
- [ ]
- [ ]
- [ ]
- [ ]
- [ ]
- [ ]
- [ ]
- [ ]

PEOPLE I NEED TO REACH OUT TO

♥
♥
♥
♥
♥

Sit Spot

A sit spot is simply a favorite place in your nearby nature that you visit regularly to cultivate awareness as you expand your senses.

By choosing one place outside that you visit over and over again, it teaches you to develop the most ancient parts of human awareness and gradually acquire enhanced sensitivity to nature.

Richard Louv talks about this by saying that nature is like *vitamins for the human mind*.

It's a way of giving yourself the mental, emotional, spiritual, and creative fuel for your own personal evolution in modern times.

People who practice Sit Spot enjoy:

- Improved sensory awareness and sensory acuity
- Enhanced critical thinking, problem solving, deductive and inductive thinking (especially when Sit Spot is associated with studies in animal tracking)
- Improved creativity
- Better naturalist skills, wildlife tracking, bird language, plant identification, etc.
- Greater capacity for releasing emotions and negative thinking through a natural state of meditation that promotes mental and physical relaxation
- Close encounters with birds, plants, trees and animals that inspire a sense of awe and wonder
- A renewed sense of happiness and joy coming from inside
- A developing sense of inner vitality and razor sharp focus
- Greater peace & joy in daily life
- A sense of connection to the past ancestry of our species and planet
- Greater flexibility of consciousness, enabling you to see life from a wider and more balanced perspective.

Humans are biologically designed to fall in love with nature, and we operate at our highest capacity when we get to live out our biological potential! Now that we've talked about why sit spot matters... let's take a closer look at how you can actually do all this!

KEEP IT SIMPLE!

One of the biggest secrets to success with having a sit spot in nature is to keep your practice routines extremely simple. Don't go far from home and visit it often. At least 3 times a week.

Remember – a sit spot is really about giving yourself the opportunity to quiet your mind and focus your senses on nature (rather than technology or any other distractions).

And this is something that can be done almost anywhere, anytime. Even 5 minutes sitting in some grass with nearby ground feeding birds is all you really need to get started and be successful. I suggest working toward at least 20 minutes each time you visit your sit spot.

In it's most basic form:

1. You just go outside.
2. Find a place in nature to sit down.
3. Practice opening your senses and observing nature.
4. If an intention is set, open your heart and see what nature has to teach you
5. Repeat as often as you can.

You will set an intention and see what nature has to teach you that day. Enjoy your time and notice how your feelings of calm seem to grow with each time you visit your sit spot!

LITHA

JUNE 20
The Season of Light, Expansion & Abundance

Overview

The Summer Solstice is the peak of the sun's power — the longest day of the year. It's a moment of abundance, clarity, and celebration. Nature is full and lush, offering her gifts generously. This is a time to honor the light within and around us, to acknowledge growth, and to take a pause to celebrate what has come to fruition. As the wheel turns, we also remember that from this point, the days will begin to shorten.

Nature's Invitation (Sit Spot Practice)

Sit in the sun and let the warmth soak into your skin. Observe how life pulses in full rhythm — birds, blossoms, bees. Reflect on your personal harvests. What have you nurtured into fullness this year? How do you radiate your inner light?

Reflective Focus:

- What am I celebrating?
- Where have I grown?
- How can I share my light with others?

Outdoor Practices:

- [ ] Watch the sunrise or sunset and offer gratitude to the sun
- [ ] Create a sun spiral from natural objects to walk or meditate in
- [ ] Sit with your back against a tree and visualize your own strength and radiance
- [ ] Make an offering of flowers or herbs to the earth in thanks

Journal

June

YEAR: _____

SUN	MON	TUE	WED	THU	FRI	SAT
○	○	○	○	○	○	○
○	○	○	○	○	○	○
○	○	○	○	○	○	○
○	○	○	○	○	○	○
○	○	○	○	○	○	○

June

PRIORITIES
1.
2.
3.

WEEK: _____
through _____

MONDAY 17
- [ ] _____
- [ ] _____
- [ ] _____
- [ ] _____
- [ ] _____
- [ ] _____

The sun does not hurry to set, and neither should you. Let your days unfold gently, filled with light and patience.

TUESDAY 17
- [ ] _____
- [ ] _____
- [ ] _____
- [ ] _____
- [ ] _____
- [ ] _____

FRIDAY 17
- [ ] _____
- [ ] _____
- [ ] _____
- [ ] _____
- [ ] _____
- [ ] _____

WEDNESDAY 17
- [ ] _____
- [ ] _____
- [ ] _____
- [ ] _____
- [ ] _____
- [ ] _____

SATURDAY 17
- [ ] _____
- [ ] _____
- [ ] _____
- [ ] _____
- [ ] _____
- [ ] _____

THURSDAY 17
- [ ] _____
- [ ] _____
- [ ] _____
- [ ] _____
- [ ] _____
- [ ] _____

SUNDAY 17
- [ ] _____
- [ ] _____
- [ ] _____
- [ ] _____
- [ ] _____
- [ ] _____

Color in one sun for each block of 17 minutes that you connect with nature per week (sit spots, mindful walks, outdoor rituals). *Aim to spend 17 minutes a day in nature.*

WEEKLY GRATITUDE

_____
_____
_____
_____
_____
_____
_____
_____
_____

MIND: *What clarity has come to me, and how can I honor it?*

BODY: *How do I feel when I let myself fully bask in the season's warmth and abundance?*

SPIRIT: *What does it mean to shine fully, and where do I hold back?*

WEEKLY NATURE SKETCH

WEEKLY TO-DO

- ○ _____
- ○ _____
- ○ _____
- ○ _____
- ○ _____
- ○ _____
- ○ _____
- ○ _____
- ○ _____
- ○ _____
- ○ _____
- ○ _____
- ○ _____
- ○ _____
- ○ _____
- ○ _____
- ○ _____
- ○ _____

MEAL PLAN

B: _____
L: _____
D: _____

B: _____
L: _____
D: _____

B: _____
L: _____
D: _____

B: _____
L: _____
D: _____

B: _____
L: _____
D: _____

B: _____
L: _____
D: _____

B: _____
L: _____
D: _____

Journal

Your Personal Wheel of Well-Being

Welcome!

This Personal Wheel is a snapshot of your life today — a map showing where you're thriving and where a little more sunlight, water, and nurturing might help you grow. Just like a tree needs sunlight, soil, and water to flourish, we too need intentional care across different areas of life.

Before You Start:

Remember that research shows spending just 17 minutes a day in nature begins to create real change in your brain, body, and spirit. As you fill out this wheel, I invite you to imagine yourself like a strong, beautiful oak tree — standing firm, growing, and reaching for the sun.

Here's how to fill it out:

1. Look at each section of your Wheel.

Each area has two parts (Personal and Business, where applicable). You'll be scoring yourself from 1 to 10:
- 1 means you feel depleted or lacking in that area — like a dry riverbed.
- 10 means you are absolutely thriving — like a lush forest after a spring rain.

2. Sections to score:

- **Spiritual Connection**
  - Personal: How connected do you feel to your own sense of spirit, inner peace, or purpose?
  - Community: How connected do you feel spiritually with others, through community, group practices, or shared values?
- **Emotional Stress Level**
  - Business: How often do you feel calm and resilient versus overwhelmed in your work life?
  - Personal: How well do you handle emotional ups and downs in your personal life?
- **Physical Health**
  - Exercise: How consistent and satisfying is your movement practice?
  - Nutrition: How nourished and energized do you feel by what you eat?
- **Financial Health**
  - Personal: How secure and in control do you feel about your personal finances?
  - Business: How stable and sustainable is your business or work income?

- ***Curiosity***
  - Personal: How often are you exploring, learning, or trying new things just for yourself?
  - Business: How often are you staying curious, growing, and innovating in your work or business life?

3. Be honest and gentle.

Nature doesn't rush her seasons, and neither should you. Today's score isn't about judgment — it's about awareness. Even a tiny acorn eventually becomes a mighty oak.

4. After scoring:

- Notice the areas that feel strong — celebrate them!
- Notice the areas that feel tender — these are invitations for gentle attention.
- Remember: Just 17 minutes a day in nature can begin to shift your energy in any of these areas. Even a walk under the trees, sitting by a garden, or feeling the breeze on your face counts.

5. Plant a Seed of Intention.

Choose one small, nurturing action to tend to the areas that feel tender as you move into the new season. Examples:
- If your Personal Spiritual Connection feels low, you might commit to sitting under a tree for five minutes each morning.
- If your Business Emotional Stress Level is high, you might block out one afternoon a week to work outside or take mindful breaks.
- If your Physical Exercise score is low, you could begin with a 10-minute nature walk after dinner each evening.
- If your Personal Finances feel strained, you could start a gratitude journal focused on non-material abundance found in nature.
- If your Curiosity in Business feels dull, you might visit a botanical garden or attend an outdoor workshop to spark new ideas.

July Wheel of Wellbeing

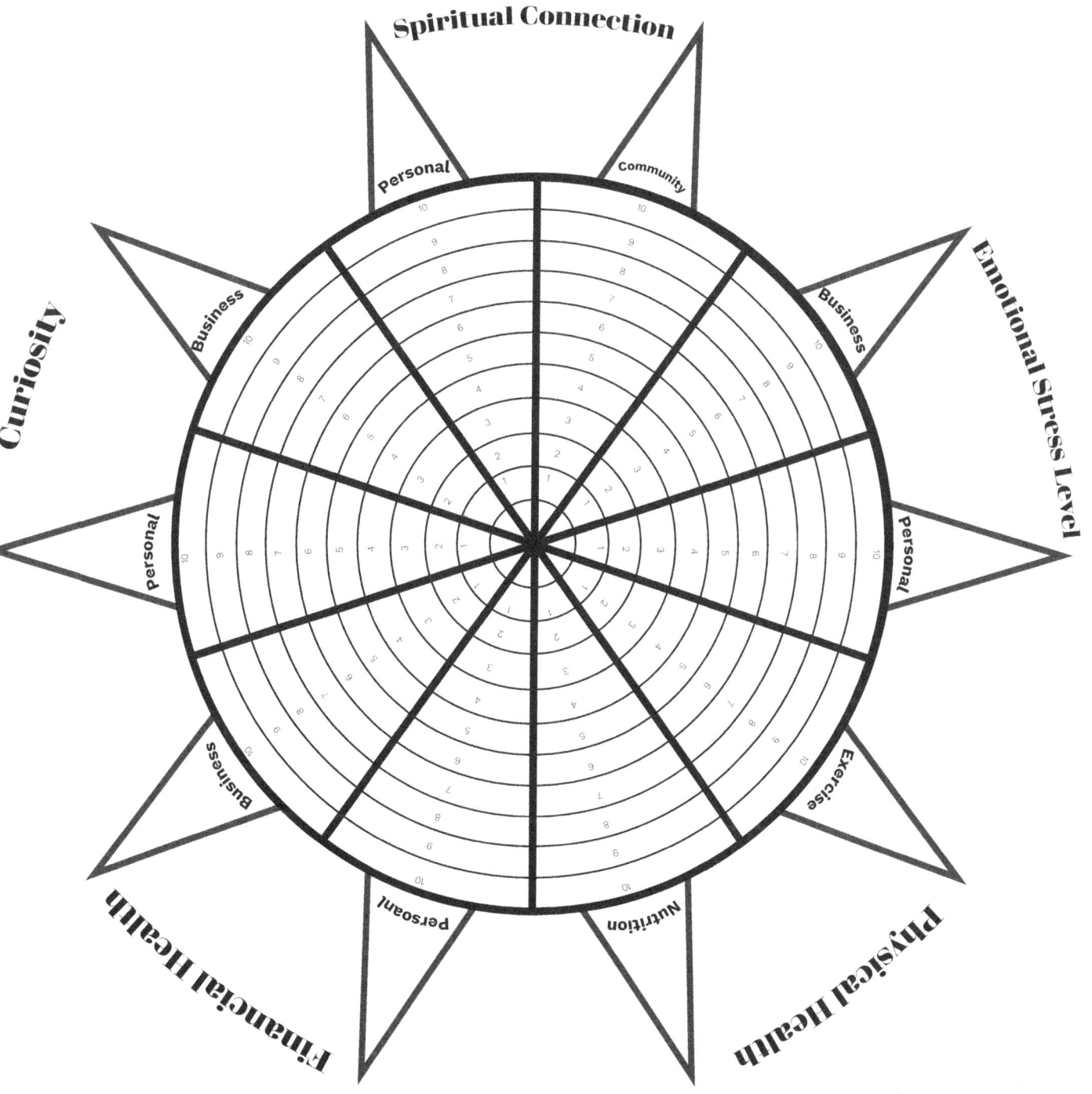

Seeds of Intention: _____
_____
_____
_____

The Phases of the Moon

NEW MOON

The New Moon is the first day of the new lunar cycle. In may perspectives, this phase is linked with the Dark Moon, consider your intentions, sow seeds, tend to the shadow dream, scheme, plot, and plan, *(This is an excellent time for shadow work, connecting with spirit, and spiritual practicing.)*

WAXING CRESCENT

As the moon grows, so can your plans and intentions. The Waxing Crescent moon is a phase approximately between two to six days old. *(Connect with the Waxing Crescent phase to build momentum, bring an action to your dreams, and begin a new process.)*

FIRST QUARTER

A First Quarter Moon is approximately between six to nine days in the lunar cycle. *(Much like the Waxing Crescent, this phase can help you work toward your goals, develop habits, and move, through processes.)*

WAXING GIBBOUS

The Waxing Gibbous moon phase is approximately between Six to thirteen days old. *(Connect with the Waxing Gibbous phase for spiritual practice and intention setting towards abundance, expansion, growth, and working toward culmination.)*

FULL MOON

The Full Moon phase is approximately between thirteen and fifteen days old. *(The Full Moon is a celebration of wholeness, release, fulfillment, sensuality, and abundance spiritual practice.)*

WANING GIBBOUS

The Waning Gibbous moon is approximately between fifteen and twenty-one days old. *(Connect with the Waning Gibbous phase to integrate the lessons of the full moon, deepen understanding, and continue to release.)*

SECOND QUARTER

The Second (Last) Quarter phase is approximately between twenty-one and twenty-three days old. *(Connect with a Last Quarter moon to support rituals with the intent of internal work. This is a great moon for working through the subconscious and shadow work.)*

WANING CRESCENT

The Waning Crescent phase is the approximately between twenty-three and twenty-seven days old. *(The Waning Crescent phase can help you clean, clear, purify, banish, and release. Under the darkening moon, connect more and more with that which is liminal and intuitive for you.)*

DARK MOON

The Dark Moon is the end of the lunar cycle before beginning again, taking place at approximately twenty-seven to twenty-nine days. *(The Dark Moon asks you to turn inward, to reflect and rest, and to banish and release anything that you're ready to let go of.)*

The Phases of the Moon
July Intention Setting

WAXING MOON
Taking Action, Building Momentum

What inspired action can I take now to move closer to my intentions?

DATE: _____

FULL MOON
Releasing, Celebrating, Acknowledging

What am I ready to celebrate, release, and honor from this cycle to make space for what's next?

DATE: _____

WANING MOON
Releasing, Letting Go

What thoughts, habits, or patterns am I ready to let go of to align more fully with my purpose?

DATE: _____

NEW MOON
Planting Seeds, Setting Goals

What intention or desire do I want to plant and nurture in the cycle ahead?

DATE: _____

July

YEAR: _____

SUN	MON	TUE	WED
○	○	○	○
○	○	○	○
○	○	○	○
○	○	○	○
○	○	○	○

FULL BLOOM CHECK-IN

Find a quiet spot outdoors near blooming flowers, tall grasses, or lush greenery. Sit comfortably and take a few deep breaths, letting yourself settle into the present moment. Look closely at the plants around you — notice their colors, shapes, and how fully alive they seem. Then gently turn your attention inward and ask yourself, **"What feels full and alive in me right now?"** Allow your thoughts and feelings to arise naturally without judgment. Take out your journal and write whatever comes up — it might be emotions, physical sensations, or moments of joy and gratitude. Let this be a celebration of your own fullness and vitality, just like the nature surrounding you.

THU	FRI	SAT
○	○	○
○	○	○
○	○	○
○	○	○
○	○	○

July

	PRIORITIES
1.	
2.	
3.	

WEEK: _____

through _____

MONDAY 17
- [ ] _____
- [ ] _____
- [ ] _____
- [ ] _____
- [ ] _____
- [ ] _____

Like flowers reaching toward the sun, open your heart fully and soak in the abundance all around you.

TUESDAY 17
- [ ] _____
- [ ] _____
- [ ] _____
- [ ] _____
- [ ] _____
- [ ] _____

FRIDAY 17
- [ ] _____
- [ ] _____
- [ ] _____
- [ ] _____
- [ ] _____
- [ ] _____

WEDNESDAY 17
- [ ] _____
- [ ] _____
- [ ] _____
- [ ] _____
- [ ] _____
- [ ] _____

SATURDAY 17
- [ ] _____
- [ ] _____
- [ ] _____
- [ ] _____
- [ ] _____
- [ ] _____

THURSDAY 17
- [ ] _____
- [ ] _____
- [ ] _____
- [ ] _____
- [ ] _____
- [ ] _____

SUNDAY 17
- [ ] _____
- [ ] _____
- [ ] _____
- [ ] _____
- [ ] _____
- [ ] _____

Color in one sun for each block of 17 minutes that you connect with nature per week (sit spots, mindful walks, outdoor rituals). *Aim to spend 17 minutes a day in nature.*

WEEKLY GRATITUDE

_____
_____
_____
_____
_____
_____
_____
_____
_____

MIND: *What clarity has come to me, and how can I honor it?*

BODY: *How do I feel when I let myself fully bask in the season's warmth and abundance?*

SPIRIT: *What does it mean to shine fully, and where do I hold back?*

WEEKLY NATURE SKETCH

WEEKLY TO-DO

- _____
- _____
- _____
- _____
- _____
- _____
- _____
- _____
- _____
- _____
- _____
- _____
- _____
- _____
- _____
- _____
- _____
- _____

MEAL PLAN

B: _____
L: _____
D: _____

B: _____
L: _____
D: _____

B: _____
L: _____
D: _____

B: _____
L: _____
D: _____

B: _____
L: _____
D: _____

B: _____
L: _____
D: _____

B: _____
L: _____
D: _____

PRIORITIES
1.
2.
3.

WEEK: _____

through _____

MONDAY ☀17
- ☐ _____
- ☐ _____
- ☐ _____
- ☐ _____
- ☐ _____
- ☐ _____
- ☐ _____

Fullness isn't about having more — it's about appreciating what is already blooming within you.

TUESDAY ☀17
- ☐ _____
- ☐ _____
- ☐ _____
- ☐ _____
- ☐ _____
- ☐ _____
- ☐ _____

FRIDAY ☀17
- ☐ _____
- ☐ _____
- ☐ _____
- ☐ _____
- ☐ _____
- ☐ _____
- ☐ _____

WEDNESDAY ☀17
- ☐ _____
- ☐ _____
- ☐ _____
- ☐ _____
- ☐ _____
- ☐ _____
- ☐ _____

SATURDAY ☀17
- ☐ _____
- ☐ _____
- ☐ _____
- ☐ _____
- ☐ _____
- ☐ _____
- ☐ _____

THURSDAY ☀17
- ☐ _____
- ☐ _____
- ☐ _____
- ☐ _____
- ☐ _____
- ☐ _____
- ☐ _____

SUNDAY ☀17
- ☐ _____
- ☐ _____
- ☐ _____
- ☐ _____
- ☐ _____
- ☐ _____
- ☐ _____

Color in one sun for each block of 17 minutes that you connect with nature per week (sit spots, mindful walks, outdoor rituals). *Aim to spend 17 minutes a day in nature.*

WEEKLY GRATITUDE

_____
_____
_____
_____
_____
_____
_____
_____

MIND: *What clarity has come to me, and how can I honor it?*

BODY: *How do I feel when I let myself fully bask in the season's warmth and abundance?*

SPIRIT: *What does it mean to shine fully, and where do I hold back?*

WEEKLY NATURE SKETCH

WEEKLY TO-DO

- ○ _____
- ○ _____
- ○ _____
- ○ _____
- ○ _____
- ○ _____
- ○ _____
- ○ _____
- ○ _____
- ○ _____
- ○ _____
- ○ _____
- ○ _____
- ○ _____
- ○ _____
- ○ _____
- ○ _____
- ○ _____

MEAL PLAN

B: _____
L: _____
D: _____

B: _____
L: _____
D: _____

B: _____
L: _____
D: _____

B: _____
L: _____
D: _____

B: _____
L: _____
D: _____

B: _____
L: _____
D: _____

B: _____
L: _____
D: _____

July

PRIORITIES
1.
2.
3.

WEEK: _____
through _____

MONDAY
- [ ] _____
- [ ] _____
- [ ] _____
- [ ] _____
- [ ] _____
- [ ] _____

In the warmth of summer, find stillness. Rest deeply, for even the brightest blooms need quiet roots.

TUESDAY
- [ ] _____
- [ ] _____
- [ ] _____
- [ ] _____
- [ ] _____
- [ ] _____

FRIDAY
- [ ] _____
- [ ] _____
- [ ] _____
- [ ] _____
- [ ] _____
- [ ] _____

WEDNESDAY
- [ ] _____
- [ ] _____
- [ ] _____
- [ ] _____
- [ ] _____
- [ ] _____

SATURDAY
- [ ] _____
- [ ] _____
- [ ] _____
- [ ] _____
- [ ] _____
- [ ] _____

THURSDAY
- [ ] _____
- [ ] _____
- [ ] _____
- [ ] _____
- [ ] _____
- [ ] _____

SUNDAY
- [ ] _____
- [ ] _____
- [ ] _____
- [ ] _____
- [ ] _____
- [ ] _____

Color in one sun for each block of 17 minutes that you connect with nature per week (sit spots, mindful walks, outdoor rituals). *Aim to spend 17 minutes a day in nature.*

WEEKLY GRATITUDE

_____
_____
_____
_____
_____
_____
_____
_____

MIND: *What clarity has come to me, and how can I honor it?*

BODY: *How do I feel when I let myself fully bask in the season's warmth and abundance?*

SPIRIT: *What does it mean to shine fully, and where do I hold back?*

WEEKLY NATURE SKETCH

WEEKLY TO-DO

- _____
- _____
- _____
- _____
- _____
- _____
- _____
- _____
- _____
- _____
- _____
- _____
- _____
- _____
- _____
- _____
- _____
- _____

MEAL PLAN

B: _____
L: _____
D: _____

B: _____
L: _____
D: _____

B: _____
L: _____
D: _____

B: _____
L: _____
D: _____

B: _____
L: _____
D: _____

B: _____
L: _____
D: _____

B: _____
L: _____
D: _____

July

PRIORITIES
1.
2.
3.

WEEK: _____

through _____

MONDAY 17
- ☐ _____
- ☐ _____
- ☐ _____
- ☐ _____
- ☐ _____
- ☐ _____

Gratitude waters the seeds of joy. Take a moment to notice what's thriving in your life today.

TUESDAY 17
- ☐ _____
- ☐ _____
- ☐ _____
- ☐ _____
- ☐ _____
- ☐ _____

FRIDAY 17
- ☐ _____
- ☐ _____
- ☐ _____
- ☐ _____
- ☐ _____
- ☐ _____

WEDNESDAY 17
- ☐ _____
- ☐ _____
- ☐ _____
- ☐ _____
- ☐ _____
- ☐ _____

SATURDAY 17
- ☐ _____
- ☐ _____
- ☐ _____
- ☐ _____
- ☐ _____
- ☐ _____

THURSDAY 17
- ☐ _____
- ☐ _____
- ☐ _____
- ☐ _____
- ☐ _____
- ☐ _____

SUNDAY 17
- ☐ _____
- ☐ _____
- ☐ _____
- ☐ _____
- ☐ _____
- ☐ _____

Color in one sun for each block of 17 minutes that you connect with nature per week (sit spots, mindful walks, outdoor rituals). *Aim to spend 17 minutes a day in nature.*

WEEKLY GRATITUDE

_____
_____
_____
_____
_____
_____
_____
_____

MIND: *What clarity has come to me, and how can I honor it?*

BODY: *How do I feel when I let myself fully bask in the season's warmth and abundance?*

SPIRIT: *What does it mean to shine fully, and where do I hold back?*

WEEKLY NATURE SKETCH

WEEKLY TO-DO

- ○ _____
- ○ _____
- ○ _____
- ○ _____
- ○ _____
- ○ _____
- ○ _____
- ○ _____
- ○ _____
- ○ _____
- ○ _____
- ○ _____
- ○ _____
- ○ _____
- ○ _____
- ○ _____
- ○ _____
- ○ _____

MEAL PLAN

B: _____
L: _____
D: _____

B: _____
L: _____
D: _____

B: _____
L: _____
D: _____

B: _____
L: _____
D: _____

B: _____
L: _____
D: _____

B: _____
L: _____
D: _____

B: _____
L: _____
D: _____

Journal

Journal

Journal

Journal

July Sit Spot Reflections

What is nature teaching me?

How am I growing into my true self?

What steps am I taking toward my soul's passion?

July Sit Spot Reflections

August Wheel of Wellbeing

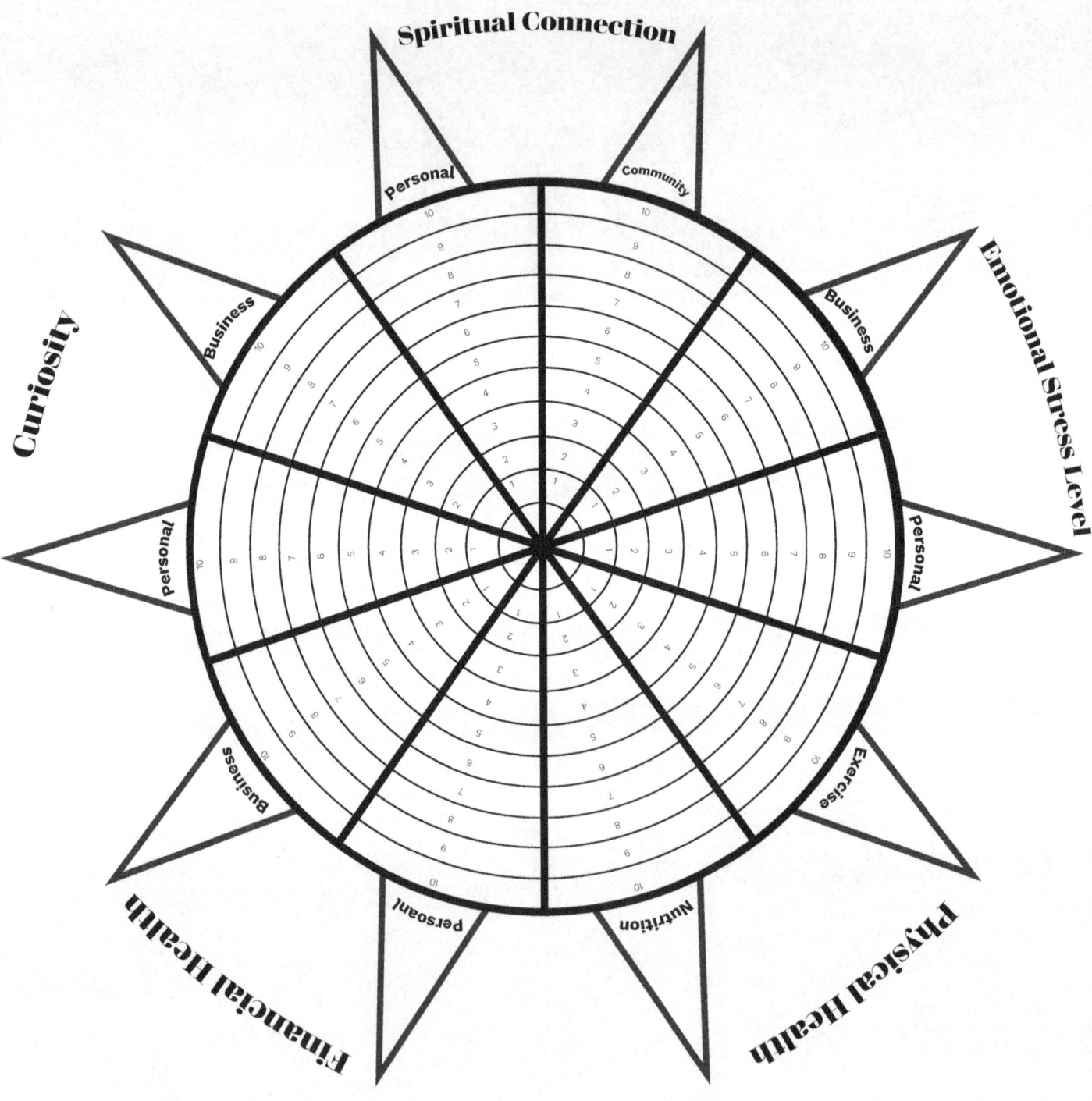

Seeds of Intention: _____
_____
_____
_____

The Phases of the Moon
August Intention Setting

WAXING MOON
Taking Action, Building Momentum

What inspired action can I take now to move closer to my intentions?

DATE: _____

FULL MOON
Releasing, Celebrating, Acknowledging

What am I ready to celebrate, release, and honor from this cycle to make space for what's next?

DATE: _____

WANING MOON
Releasing, Letting Go

What thoughts, habits, or patterns am I ready to let go of to align more fully with my purpose?

DATE: _____

NEW MOON
Planting Seeds, Setting Goals

What intention or desire do I want to plant and nurture in the cycle ahead?

DATE: _____

Journal

LAMMAS

AUGUST 1

The Season of Harvest, Gratitude & Preparation

Overview

Lammas marks the beginning of the harvest season and sits at the peak of summer's abundance. It's a time to celebrate the fruits of your labor, both visible and unseen. Traditionally, Lammas honors the first grain harvest—bread made from wheat, rye, or barley—symbolizing nourishment, gratitude, and community. Nature is heavy with ripening fruits, golden fields, and the hum of busy bees. This season invites us to slow down, appreciate what we've grown, and prepare our hearts for the coming transition. It's a moment to honor both abundance and the wisdom of letting go.

Nature's Invitation (Sit Spot Practice)

Find a spot near ripe fruit trees, grain fields, or gardens. Sit quietly and tune into the richness around you—the weight of fruit on branches, the scent of ripeness, the buzz of pollinators. Breathe deeply and feel the fullness of the season in your body. Notice what gratitude arises and what your heart is ready to release in this time of plenty.

Reflective Focus:

- What have I nurtured and brought to fruition this year?
- How can I celebrate my own growth and effort?
- What am I ready to release as I prepare for the next phase?

Outdoor Practices:

- [ ] Bake or share bread or seasonal fruit with someone you love, honoring the harvest
- [ ] Take a slow "harvest walk" collecting fallen leaves, seeds, or stones as symbols of your journey
- [ ] Journal your gratitude for the visible and invisible abundance in your life
- [ ] Create a simple altar or offering with harvest items, giving thanks to the earth

August

YEAR: _____

SUN	MON	TUE	WED
○	○	○	○
○	○	○	○
○	○	○	○
○	○	○	○
○	○	○	○

SLOW WALKING MEDITATION

Choose a natural place to walk—this could be a park, garden, or a quiet path. Begin walking at about half your usual pace. As you move slowly, bring your full attention to your senses. Notice the sounds around you — the buzzing of insects, the rustling of leaves, the chirping of birds. Feel the warmth of the sun or the coolness of the breeze on your skin. Observe the colors and textures of ripening fruits, leaves, or flowers. If your mind wanders, gently bring it back to these sensations. Allow your body to slow down and move in harmony with the natural rhythm around you. After your walk, sit and journal or quietly reflect on how this slower pace shifted your experience.

THU	FRI	SAT
○	○	○
○	○	○
○	○	○
○	○	○
○	○	○

August

PRIORITIES
1.
2.
3.

WEEK: _____
through _____

MONDAY

- [ ] _____
- [ ] _____
- [ ] _____
- [ ] _____
- [ ] _____
- [ ] _____
- [ ] _____

The earth invites us to slow our pace — to walk lightly, breathe deeply, and savor every step.

TUESDAY

- [ ] _____
- [ ] _____
- [ ] _____
- [ ] _____
- [ ] _____
- [ ] _____
- [ ] _____

FRIDAY

- [ ] _____
- [ ] _____
- [ ] _____
- [ ] _____
- [ ] _____
- [ ] _____
- [ ] _____

WEDNESDAY

- [ ] _____
- [ ] _____
- [ ] _____
- [ ] _____
- [ ] _____
- [ ] _____
- [ ] _____

SATURDAY

- [ ] _____
- [ ] _____
- [ ] _____
- [ ] _____
- [ ] _____
- [ ] _____
- [ ] _____

THURSDAY

- [ ] _____
- [ ] _____
- [ ] _____
- [ ] _____
- [ ] _____
- [ ] _____
- [ ] _____

SUNDAY

- [ ] _____
- [ ] _____
- [ ] _____
- [ ] _____
- [ ] _____
- [ ] _____
- [ ] _____

Color in one sun for each block of 17 minutes that you connect with nature per week (sit spots, mindful walks, outdoor rituals). *Aim to spend 17 minutes a day in nature.*

WEEKLY GRATITUDE

_____
_____
_____
_____
_____
_____
_____
_____

MIND: *What clarity has come to me, and how can I honor it?*

BODY: *How do I feel when I let myself fully bask in the season's warmth and abundance?*

SPIRIT: *What does it mean to shine fully, and where do I hold back?*

WEEKLY NATURE SKETCH

WEEKLY TO-DO

- _____
- _____
- _____
- _____
- _____
- _____
- _____
- _____
- _____
- _____
- _____
- _____
- _____
- _____
- _____
- _____
- _____
- _____

MEAL PLAN

B: _____
L: _____
D: _____

B: _____
L: _____
D: _____

B: _____
L: _____
D: _____

B: _____
L: _____
D: _____

B: _____
L: _____
D: _____

B: _____
L: _____
D: _____

B: _____
L: _____
D: _____

B: _____
L: _____
D: _____

August

PRIORITIES
1.
2.
3.

WEEK: _____
through _____

MONDAY 17
- [ ] _____
- [ ] _____
- [ ] _____
- [ ] _____
- [ ] _____
- [ ] _____

Harvest your lessons and your love. Celebrate the richness of your journey, no matter how small the steps.

TUESDAY 17
- [ ] _____
- [ ] _____
- [ ] _____
- [ ] _____
- [ ] _____
- [ ] _____

FRIDAY 17
- [ ] _____
- [ ] _____
- [ ] _____
- [ ] _____
- [ ] _____
- [ ] _____

WEDNESDAY 17
- [ ] _____
- [ ] _____
- [ ] _____
- [ ] _____
- [ ] _____
- [ ] _____

SATURDAY 17
- [ ] _____
- [ ] _____
- [ ] _____
- [ ] _____
- [ ] _____
- [ ] _____

THURSDAY 17
- [ ] _____
- [ ] _____
- [ ] _____
- [ ] _____
- [ ] _____
- [ ] _____

SUNDAY 17
- [ ] _____
- [ ] _____
- [ ] _____
- [ ] _____
- [ ] _____
- [ ] _____

Color in one sun for each block of 17 minutes that you connect with nature per week (sit spots, mindful walks, outdoor rituals). *Aim to spend 17 minutes a day in nature.*

WEEKLY GRATITUDE

_____
_____
_____
_____
_____
_____
_____
_____
_____

MIND: *What clarity has come to me, and how can I honor it?*

BODY: *How do I feel when I let myself fully bask in the season's warmth and abundance?*

SPIRIT: *What does it mean to shine fully, and where do I hold back?*

WEEKLY NATURE SKETCH

WEEKLY TO-DO

- _____
- _____
- _____
- _____
- _____
- _____
- _____
- _____
- _____
- _____
- _____
- _____
- _____
- _____
- _____
- _____
- _____
- _____

MEAL PLAN

B: _____
L: _____
D: _____

B: _____
L: _____
D: _____

B: _____
L: _____
D: _____

B: _____
L: _____
D: _____

B: _____
L: _____
D: _____

B: _____
L: _____
D: _____

B: _____
L: _____
D: _____

August

PRIORITIES
1.
2.
3.

WEEK: _____
through _____

MONDAY
17
- [ ] _____
- [ ] _____
- [ ] _____
- [ ] _____
- [ ] _____
- [ ] _____

Like the golden fields ready for gathering, prepare your heart to receive all the good that's ripe and waiting.

TUESDAY
17
- [ ] _____
- [ ] _____
- [ ] _____
- [ ] _____
- [ ] _____
- [ ] _____

FRIDAY
17
- [ ] _____
- [ ] _____
- [ ] _____
- [ ] _____
- [ ] _____
- [ ] _____

WEDNESDAY
17
- [ ] _____
- [ ] _____
- [ ] _____
- [ ] _____
- [ ] _____
- [ ] _____

SATURDAY
17
- [ ] _____
- [ ] _____
- [ ] _____
- [ ] _____
- [ ] _____
- [ ] _____

THURSDAY
17
- [ ] _____
- [ ] _____
- [ ] _____
- [ ] _____
- [ ] _____
- [ ] _____

SUNDAY
17
- [ ] _____
- [ ] _____
- [ ] _____
- [ ] _____
- [ ] _____
- [ ] _____

Color in one sun for each block of 17 minutes that you connect with nature per week (sit spots, mindful walks, outdoor rituals). *Aim to spend 17 minutes a day in nature.*

WEEKLY GRATITUDE

_____
_____
_____
_____
_____
_____
_____
_____
_____

MIND: *What clarity has come to me, and how can I honor it?*

BODY: *How do I feel when I let myself fully bask in the season's warmth and abundance?*

SPIRIT: *What does it mean to shine fully, and where do I hold back?*

WEEKLY NATURE SKETCH

WEEKLY TO-DO

- _____
- _____
- _____
- _____
- _____
- _____
- _____
- _____
- _____
- _____
- _____
- _____
- _____
- _____
- _____
- _____
- _____

MEAL PLAN

B: _____
L: _____
D: _____

B: _____
L: _____
D: _____

B: _____
L: _____
D: _____

B: _____
L: _____
D: _____

B: _____
L: _____
D: _____

B: _____
L: _____
D: _____

B: _____
L: _____
D: _____

August

PRIORITIES
1.
2.
3.

WEEK: _____
through _____

MONDAY 17

- [ ] _____
- [ ] _____
- [ ] _____
- [ ] _____
- [ ] _____
- [ ] _____

Even the sun must dip below the horizon. Trust the rhythm of letting go as you prepare for new beginnings.

TUESDAY 17

- [ ] _____
- [ ] _____
- [ ] _____
- [ ] _____
- [ ] _____
- [ ] _____

FRIDAY 17

- [ ] _____
- [ ] _____
- [ ] _____
- [ ] _____
- [ ] _____
- [ ] _____

WEDNESDAY 17

- [ ] _____
- [ ] _____
- [ ] _____
- [ ] _____
- [ ] _____
- [ ] _____

SATURDAY 17

- [ ] _____
- [ ] _____
- [ ] _____
- [ ] _____
- [ ] _____
- [ ] _____

THURSDAY 17

- [ ] _____
- [ ] _____
- [ ] _____
- [ ] _____
- [ ] _____
- [ ] _____

SUNDAY 17

- [ ] _____
- [ ] _____
- [ ] _____
- [ ] _____
- [ ] _____
- [ ] _____

Color in one sun for each block of 17 minutes that you connect with nature per week (sit spots, mindful walks, outdoor rituals). *Aim to spend 17 minutes a day in nature.*

WEEKLY GRATITUDE

_____
_____
_____
_____
_____
_____
_____
_____
_____

MIND: *What clarity has come to me, and how can I honor it?*

BODY: *How do I feel when I let myself fully bask in the season's warmth and abundance?*

SPIRIT: *What does it mean to shine fully, and where do I hold back?*

WEEKLY NATURE SKETCH

WEEKLY TO-DO

- ☐ _____
- ☐ _____
- ☐ _____
- ☐ _____
- ☐ _____
- ☐ _____
- ☐ _____
- ☐ _____
- ☐ _____
- ☐ _____
- ☐ _____
- ☐ _____
- ☐ _____
- ☐ _____
- ☐ _____
- ☐ _____
- ☐ _____
- ☐ _____
- ☐ _____

MEAL PLAN

B: _____
L: _____
D: _____

B: _____
L: _____
D: _____

B: _____
L: _____
D: _____

B: _____
L: _____
D: _____

B: _____
L: _____
D: _____

B: _____
L: _____
D: _____

B: _____
L: _____
D: _____

August

PRIORITIES
1.
2.
3.

WEEK: _____

through _____

You are allowed to slow down, even in the fullness of life. Growth is not always in the doing— sometimes it's in the being.

MONDAY — 17

- [ ] _____
- [ ] _____
- [ ] _____
- [ ] _____
- [ ] _____
- [ ] _____

TUESDAY — 17

- [ ] _____
- [ ] _____
- [ ] _____
- [ ] _____
- [ ] _____
- [ ] _____

WEDNESDAY — 17

- [ ] _____
- [ ] _____
- [ ] _____
- [ ] _____
- [ ] _____
- [ ] _____

THURSDAY — 17

- [ ] _____
- [ ] _____
- [ ] _____
- [ ] _____
- [ ] _____
- [ ] _____

FRIDAY — 17

- [ ] _____
- [ ] _____
- [ ] _____
- [ ] _____
- [ ] _____
- [ ] _____

SATURDAY — 17

- [ ] _____
- [ ] _____
- [ ] _____
- [ ] _____
- [ ] _____
- [ ] _____

SUNDAY — 17

- [ ] _____
- [ ] _____
- [ ] _____
- [ ] _____
- [ ] _____
- [ ] _____

Color in one sun for each block of 17 minutes that you connect with nature per week (sit spots, mindful walks, outdoor rituals). *Aim to spend 17 minutes a day in nature.*

WEEKLY GRATITUDE

_____
_____
_____
_____
_____
_____
_____
_____
_____

MIND: *What clarity has come to me, and how can I honor it?*

BODY: *How do I feel when I let myself fully bask in the season's warmth and abundance?*

SPIRIT: *What does it mean to shine fully, and where do I hold back?*

WEEKLY NATURE SKETCH

WEEKLY TO-DO

- ○ _____
- ○ _____
- ○ _____
- ○ _____
- ○ _____
- ○ _____
- ○ _____
- ○ _____
- ○ _____
- ○ _____
- ○ _____
- ○ _____
- ○ _____
- ○ _____
- ○ _____
- ○ _____
- ○ _____

MEAL PLAN

B: _____
L: _____
D: _____

B: _____
L: _____
D: _____

B: _____
L: _____
D: _____

B: _____
L: _____
D: _____

B: _____
L: _____
D: _____

B: _____
L: _____
D: _____

B: _____
L: _____
D: _____

Journal

Journal

Journal

Journal

August
Sit Spot
REFLECTIONS

What is nature teaching me?

How am I growing into my true self?

What steps am I taking toward my soul's passion?

August Sit Spot Reflections

MABON

SEPTEMBER 22

The Season of Balance, Reflection & Gratitude

Overview

Mabon, the Autumn Equinox, is a sacred time of balance—day and night stand equal, light and dark hold hands. It marks the shift from high summer into the cooling embrace of fall. The trees begin their colorful transformation, and the earth's energy slows, inviting reflection and restoration. Mabon is a season of thanksgiving, honoring the harvest's completion and recognizing the cycle of reciprocity between giving and receiving. It's a time to find equilibrium in your own life—balancing work and rest, light and shadow, doing and being.

Nature's Invitation (Sit Spot Practice)

Sit quietly beneath a tree that's beginning to show its fall colors. Close your eyes and breathe in the crisp, shifting air. Notice the balance of warmth and coolness, light and shadow around you. Reflect on what parts of your life need more balance and harmony. Allow yourself to feel gratitude for what has been harvested and gentle acceptance for what is ending.

Reflective Focus:

- Where do I feel balanced in my life? Where do I feel out of alignment?
- What do I need to nurture or release to restore harmony?
- How can I honor both light and dark within myself?

Outdoor Practices:

- [ ] Take a mindful walk noticing the changing colors, sounds, and smells of autumn
- [ ] Create a gratitude list inspired by nature's gifts this season
- [ ] Practice a "balancing breath" meditation outside, inhaling calm and exhaling tension
- [ ] Gather fallen leaves or acorns and create a mandala or altar symbolizing balance and gratitude

Journal

Early Fall
Season Mindset

One thing in nature that inspires or excites me this season is...

A positive phrase I can repeat to myself while grounded in nature is...

Someone who needs my full presence and energy this season is...

A situation that might stress me out or trip me up this season could be...

> *... and I will take a moment in nature to breathe, observe, or connect before responding as my best self.*

Someone I could surprise with a nature-inspired note, gift, or moment of appreciation is...

One action I could take this season to embody excellence or bring joy to my environment is…

One bold step I could take this season that mirrors nature's courage and resilience is…

If I were a guide walking alongside myself in nature, I would encourage myself with this…

I would end this season feeling proud if I make sure to spend time appreciating the small, beautiful details in my life, just like noticing a flower or sunset.

The big picture I have to keep in mind this season is that I am growing, like the cycles of nature, steadily towards…

September Wheel of Wellbeing

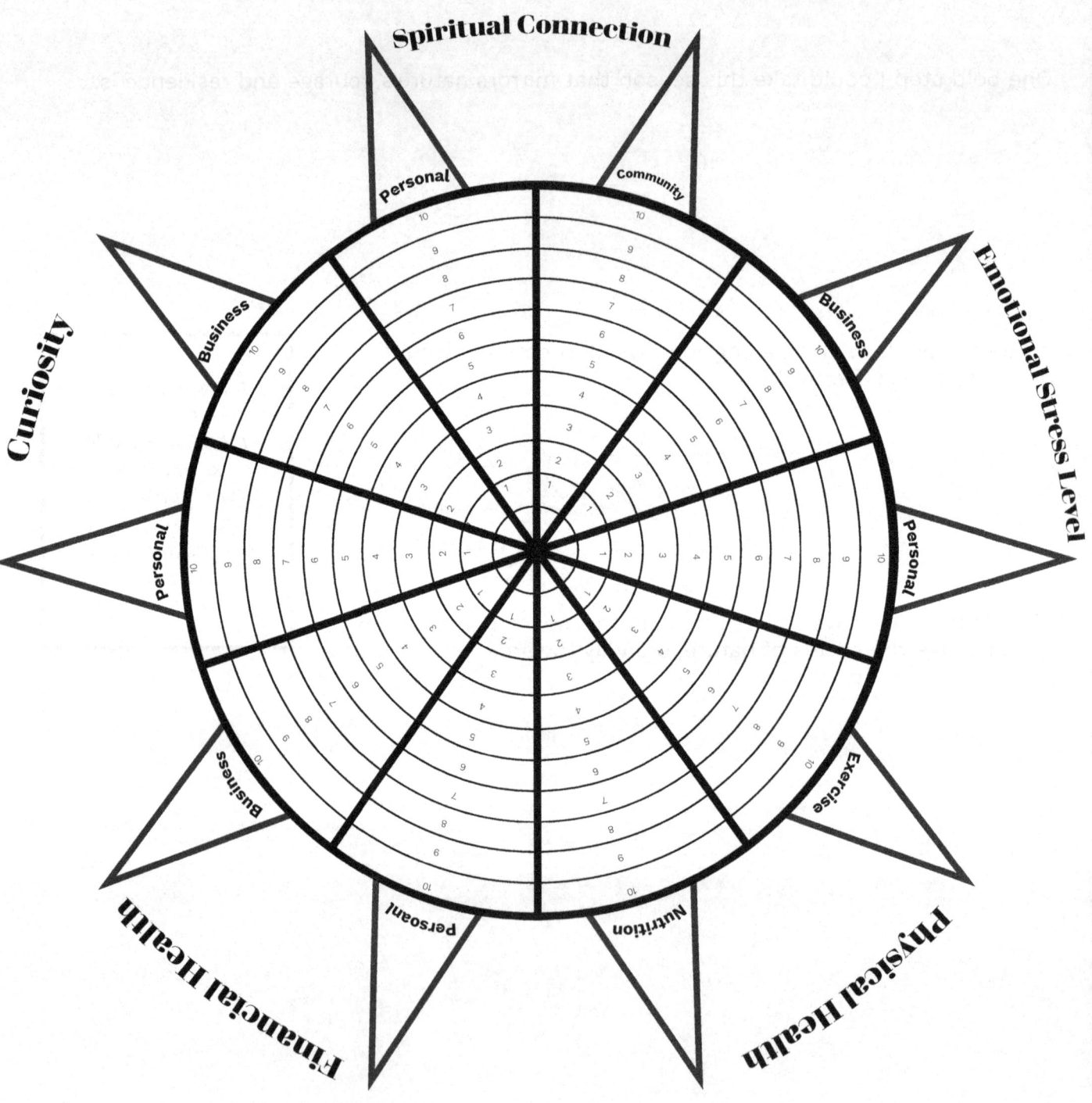

Seeds of Intention: _____

_____

_____

_____

The Phases of the Moon
September Intention Setting

WAXING MOON
Taking Action, Building Momentum

What inspired action can I take now to move closer to my intentions?

DATE: _____

FULL MOON
Releasing, Celebrating, Acknowledging

What am I ready to celebrate, release, and honor from this cycle to make space for what's next?

DATE: _____

WANING MOON
Releasing, Letting Go

What thoughts, habits, or patterns am I ready to let go of to align more fully with my purpose?

DATE: _____

NEW MOON
Planting Seeds, Setting Goals

What intention or desire do I want to plant and nurture in the cycle ahead?

DATE: _____

September

YEAR: _____

SUN	MON	TUE	WED
○	○	○	○
○	○	○	○
○	○	○	○
○	○	○	○
○	○	○	○

NATURE'S PACE JOURNALING

Find a comfortable sit spot outdoors where you can be still for at least 10–15 minutes. This could be beneath a tree, on a bench, or a quiet patch of earth. Close your eyes and take several deep breaths to settle your mind. When you feel calm, ask yourself quietly or aloud, **"What would it look like to move through life like this season — slowly, intentionally, and without rush?"** Notice any images, feelings, or thoughts that come up. What changes might you make in your daily life to honor this slower rhythm? When you're ready, open your journal and write down your reflections. Consider ways you can carry this mindful, unhurried energy with you as the season shifts toward fall.

THU	FRI	SAT
○	○	○
○	○	○
○	○	○
○	○	○
○	○	○

September

PRIORITIES
1.
2.
3.

WEEK: _____
through _____

Balance is found in embracing both light and shadow — the fullness of what is, and the grace of release.

MONDAY 17
- [ ] _____
- [ ] _____
- [ ] _____
- [ ] _____
- [ ] _____
- [ ] _____

TUESDAY 17
- [ ] _____
- [ ] _____
- [ ] _____
- [ ] _____
- [ ] _____
- [ ] _____

WEDNESDAY 17
- [ ] _____
- [ ] _____
- [ ] _____
- [ ] _____
- [ ] _____
- [ ] _____

THURSDAY 17
- [ ] _____
- [ ] _____
- [ ] _____
- [ ] _____
- [ ] _____
- [ ] _____

FRIDAY 17
- [ ] _____
- [ ] _____
- [ ] _____
- [ ] _____
- [ ] _____
- [ ] _____

SATURDAY 17
- [ ] _____
- [ ] _____
- [ ] _____
- [ ] _____
- [ ] _____
- [ ] _____

SUNDAY 17
- [ ] _____
- [ ] _____
- [ ] _____
- [ ] _____
- [ ] _____
- [ ] _____

Color in one sun for each block of 17 minutes that you connect with nature per week (sit spots, mindful walks, outdoor rituals). *Aim to spend 17 minutes a day in nature.*

WEEKLY GRATITUDE

_____
_____
_____
_____
_____
_____
_____
_____
_____

MIND: *What clarity has come to me, and how can I honor it?*

BODY: *How do I feel when I let myself fully bask in the season's warmth and abundance?*

SPIRIT: *What does it mean to shine fully, and where do I hold back?*

WEEKLY NATURE SKETCH

WEEKLY TO-DO

- _____
- _____
- _____
- _____
- _____
- _____
- _____
- _____
- _____
- _____
- _____
- _____
- _____
- _____
- _____
- _____
- _____
- _____
- _____

MEAL PLAN

B: _____
L: _____
D: _____

B: _____
L: _____
D: _____

B: _____
L: _____
D: _____

B: _____
L: _____
D: _____

B: _____
L: _____
D: _____

B: _____
L: _____
D: _____

B: _____
L: _____
D: _____

September

PRIORITIES
1.
2.
3.

WEEK: _____
through _____

MONDAY 17
- ☐ _____
- ☐ _____
- ☐ _____
- ☐ _____
- ☐ _____
- ☐ _____

As leaves begin to turn, so can you. Change is a gentle invitation, not a demand.

TUESDAY 17
- ☐ _____
- ☐ _____
- ☐ _____
- ☐ _____
- ☐ _____
- ☐ _____

FRIDAY 17
- ☐ _____
- ☐ _____
- ☐ _____
- ☐ _____
- ☐ _____
- ☐ _____

WEDNESDAY 17
- ☐ _____
- ☐ _____
- ☐ _____
- ☐ _____
- ☐ _____
- ☐ _____

SATURDAY 17
- ☐ _____
- ☐ _____
- ☐ _____
- ☐ _____
- ☐ _____
- ☐ _____

THURSDAY 17
- ☐ _____
- ☐ _____
- ☐ _____
- ☐ _____
- ☐ _____
- ☐ _____

SUNDAY 17
- ☐ _____
- ☐ _____
- ☐ _____
- ☐ _____
- ☐ _____
- ☐ _____

Color in one sun for each block of 17 minutes that you connect with nature per week (sit spots, mindful walks, outdoor rituals). *Aim to spend 17 minutes a day in nature.*

WEEKLY GRATITUDE

_____
_____
_____
_____
_____
_____
_____
_____

MIND: *What clarity has come to me, and how can I honor it?*

BODY: *How do I feel when I let myself fully bask in the season's warmth and abundance?*

SPIRIT: *What does it mean to shine fully, and where do I hold back?*

WEEKLY NATURE SKETCH

WEEKLY TO-DO

- ○ _____
- ○ _____
- ○ _____
- ○ _____
- ○ _____
- ○ _____
- ○ _____
- ○ _____
- ○ _____
- ○ _____
- ○ _____
- ○ _____
- ○ _____
- ○ _____
- ○ _____
- ○ _____
- ○ _____
- ○ _____

MEAL PLAN

B: _____
L: _____
D: _____

B: _____
L: _____
D: _____

B: _____
L: _____
D: _____

B: _____
L: _____
D: _____

B: _____
L: _____
D: _____

B: _____
L: _____
D: _____

B: _____
L: _____
D: _____

September

PRIORITIES
1.
2.
3.

WEEK: _____
through _____

MONDAY
☐ _____
☐ _____
☐ _____
☐ _____
☐ _____
☐ _____
☐ _____

Moving with the season means moving with kindness toward yourself — honoring your own natural pace.

TUESDAY
☐ _____
☐ _____
☐ _____
☐ _____
☐ _____
☐ _____
☐ _____

FRIDAY
☐ _____
☐ _____
☐ _____
☐ _____
☐ _____
☐ _____
☐ _____

WEDNESDAY
☐ _____
☐ _____
☐ _____
☐ _____
☐ _____
☐ _____
☐ _____

SATURDAY
☐ _____
☐ _____
☐ _____
☐ _____
☐ _____
☐ _____
☐ _____

THURSDAY
☐ _____
☐ _____
☐ _____
☐ _____
☐ _____
☐ _____
☐ _____

SUNDAY
☐ _____
☐ _____
☐ _____
☐ _____
☐ _____
☐ _____
☐ _____

Color in one sun for each block of 17 minutes that you connect with nature per week (sit spots, mindful walks, outdoor rituals). *Aim to spend 17 minutes a day in nature.*

WEEKLY GRATITUDE

_____
_____
_____
_____
_____
_____
_____
_____
_____

MIND: *What clarity has come to me, and how can I honor it?*

BODY: *How do I feel when I let myself fully bask in the season's warmth and abundance?*

SPIRIT: *What does it mean to shine fully, and where do I hold back?*

WEEKLY NATURE SKETCH

WEEKLY TO-DO

- ○ _____
- ○ _____
- ○ _____
- ○ _____
- ○ _____
- ○ _____
- ○ _____
- ○ _____
- ○ _____
- ○ _____
- ○ _____
- ○ _____
- ○ _____
- ○ _____
- ○ _____
- ○ _____
- ○ _____
- ○ _____

MEAL PLAN

B: _____
L: _____
D: _____

B: _____
L: _____
D: _____

B: _____
L: _____
D: _____

B: _____
L: _____
D: _____

B: _____
L: _____
D: _____

B: _____
L: _____
D: _____

B: _____
L: _____
D: _____

September

PRIORITIES
1.
2.
3.

WEEK: _____
through _____

MONDAY 17
- [ ] _____
- [ ] _____
- [ ] _____
- [ ] _____
- [ ] _____
- [ ] _____

The beauty of transition lies in the trust that endings hold space for new growth to begin.

TUESDAY 17
- [ ] _____
- [ ] _____
- [ ] _____
- [ ] _____
- [ ] _____
- [ ] _____

FRIDAY 17
- [ ] _____
- [ ] _____
- [ ] _____
- [ ] _____
- [ ] _____
- [ ] _____

WEDNESDAY 17
- [ ] _____
- [ ] _____
- [ ] _____
- [ ] _____
- [ ] _____
- [ ] _____

SATURDAY 17
- [ ] _____
- [ ] _____
- [ ] _____
- [ ] _____
- [ ] _____
- [ ] _____

THURSDAY 17
- [ ] _____
- [ ] _____
- [ ] _____
- [ ] _____
- [ ] _____
- [ ] _____

SUNDAY 17
- [ ] _____
- [ ] _____
- [ ] _____
- [ ] _____
- [ ] _____
- [ ] _____

Color in one sun for each block of 17 minutes that you connect with nature per week (sit spots, mindful walks, outdoor rituals). *Aim to spend 17 minutes a day in nature.*

WEEKLY GRATITUDE

_____
_____
_____
_____
_____
_____
_____
_____

MIND: *What clarity has come to me, and how can I honor it?*

BODY: *How do I feel when I let myself fully bask in the season's warmth and abundance?*

SPIRIT: *What does it mean to shine fully, and where do I hold back?*

WEEKLY NATURE SKETCH

WEEKLY TO-DO

- _____
- _____
- _____
- _____
- _____
- _____
- _____
- _____
- _____
- _____
- _____
- _____
- _____
- _____
- _____
- _____
- _____
- _____

MEAL PLAN

B: _____
L: _____
D: _____

B: _____
L: _____
D: _____

B: _____
L: _____
D: _____

B: _____
L: _____
D: _____

B: _____
L: _____
D: _____

B: _____
L: _____
D: _____

B: _____
L: _____
D: _____

September

WEEK: _____
through _____

MONDAY | 17

- [ ] _____
- [ ] _____
- [ ] _____
- [ ] _____
- [ ] _____
- [ ] _____

PRIORITIES
1.
2.
3.

Let the falling leaves remind you: it's okay to release what no longer serves. There is wisdom in the letting go.

TUESDAY | 17

- [ ] _____
- [ ] _____
- [ ] _____
- [ ] _____
- [ ] _____
- [ ] _____

FRIDAY | 17

- [ ] _____
- [ ] _____
- [ ] _____
- [ ] _____
- [ ] _____
- [ ] _____

WEDNESDAY | 17

- [ ] _____
- [ ] _____
- [ ] _____
- [ ] _____
- [ ] _____
- [ ] _____

SATURDAY | 17

- [ ] _____
- [ ] _____
- [ ] _____
- [ ] _____
- [ ] _____
- [ ] _____

THURSDAY | 17

- [ ] _____
- [ ] _____
- [ ] _____
- [ ] _____
- [ ] _____
- [ ] _____

SUNDAY | 17

- [ ] _____
- [ ] _____
- [ ] _____
- [ ] _____
- [ ] _____
- [ ] _____

Color in one sun for each block of 17 minutes that you connect with nature per week (sit spots, mindful walks, outdoor rituals). *Aim to spend 17 minutes a day in nature.*

WEEKLY GRATITUDE

_____
_____
_____
_____
_____
_____
_____
_____

MIND: *What clarity has come to me, and how can I honor it?*

BODY: *How do I feel when I let myself fully bask in the season's warmth and abundance?*

SPIRIT: *What does it mean to shine fully, and where do I hold back?*

WEEKLY NATURE SKETCH

WEEKLY TO-DO

- ○ _____
- ○ _____
- ○ _____
- ○ _____
- ○ _____
- ○ _____
- ○ _____
- ○ _____
- ○ _____
- ○ _____
- ○ _____
- ○ _____
- ○ _____
- ○ _____
- ○ _____
- ○ _____
- ○ _____

MEAL PLAN

B: _____
L: _____
D: _____

B: _____
L: _____
D: _____

B: _____
L: _____
D: _____

B: _____
L: _____
D: _____

B: _____
L: _____
D: _____

B: _____
L: _____
D: _____

B: _____
L: _____
D: _____

Journal

Journal

Journal

Journal

September
Sit Spot
REFLECTIONS

What is nature teaching me?

How am I growing into my true self?

What steps am I taking toward my soul's passion?

September Sit Spot Reflections

Seasonal Scorecard

Rate yourself (1-5) on these nature-connected high-performance habits.
The goal is mindfulness, not perfection.

① ② ③ ④ ⑤ **CLARITY**

I aligned with my inner wisdom and grounded my intentions by spending time in nature's stillness this season.

① ② ③ ④ ⑤ **PRODUCTIVITY**

I focused on what mattered most, moving with the natural flow of the day and allowing space for calm, presence, and nature's guidance.

① ② ③ ④ ⑤ **ENERGY**

I honored my mental, physical, and emotional energy by following natural rhythms — embracing light, rest, movement, and time outdoors.

① ② ③ ④ ⑤ **CONNECTION**

I nurtured relationships with others and with the living world around me — pausing to listen, notice, and be fully present in nature's embrace.

① ② ③ ④ ⑤ **PURPOSE**

I showed up as my truest self, drawing inspiration from the cycles, seasons, and wisdom of the Earth.

① ② ③ ④ ⑤ **COURAGE**

I expressed my authentic self with honesty and resilience, like nature itself — unafraid to stand in my truth and beauty.

Summer & Early Fall
Season Reflection

Think back on the last 3 months and answer...

A moment I truly appreciated or felt gratitude in nature last season was...

A situation or task I handled well, with calmness and balance, was...

Something I realized or learned from observing nature or being in a natural setting was...

I could have made last season even better if I had paused to notice...

Something that could have helped me feel more connected to others or to the natural world last season would have been...

If I were reflecting with myself at a sit spot in nature, I would tell myself this about my season...

Nature Pyramid

Awe

Yearly Nature:
Go Somewhere New

Monthly Trips:
Support Your State Parks

Weekly Exploration:
Visit a Local Nature Area and Explore

Apple-a-Day Nature:
Daily Trips to Your Own Nearby Nature

Discover the Power of Nature with Inner-NATURALIST

Nature has the power to restore, rejuvenate, and inspire. By incorporating nature into your daily routine, you can transform your well-being. Follow the Nature Pyramid to bring more wholeness and joy into your life:

- **Apple-a-Day Nature: Daily Nearby Nature**
    - Spend 5-10 minutes daily in your backyard, local park, or a tree-lined street.
    - Boost your mood and reduce stress with just 5 minutes outdoors.
    - Example: Start your day with coffee on your porch, listening to birds and feeling the breeze.

- **Weekly Exploration: Visit a Local Nature Area**
    - Explore local parks, trails, or nature reserves weekly.
    - Disconnect from daily life and reconnect with yourself.
    - Example: Hike at your nearest state park or take a scenic bike ride on Sundays.

- **Monthly Trips: Support Your National & State Parks**
    - Commit to a monthly trip to a state or national park.
    - Experience different environments for reflection and renewal.
    - Example: Plan a weekend getaway to a nearby state park for hiking, camping, and relaxation.

- **Yearly Nature: Experience Awe in New Places**
    - Take a yearly trip to an awe-inspiring destination.
    - Reflect, grow, and transform in the wonders of nature.
    - Example: Join Inner-NATURALIST for an awe inspiring retreat

Why Nature Connected Coaching?

- Use nature as a tool for personal growth and healing.
- Overcome challenges, reduce stress, and bring more joy into your life.
- Learn to harness the cycles and seasons of nature.

Join Us on the Journey to Wholeness and Joy!

Explore our website: www.inner-naturalist.com

Email us: yourinnernaturalist@gmail.com

Journal

Journal

Journal

Journal

Journal

Journal

Journal

Journal

Journal

Journal

Journal

Journal

Journal

Journal

Journal

Journal

ABOUT THE AUTHOR

Hi, I'm Lari Jo—a Nature Connected Transformational Coach, a lifelong lover of the outdoors, and someone who found her way back to wholeness through the wisdom of the natural world.

My path here hasn't been straight. Like so many of us, I've walked through seasons of grief, stress, burnout, and deep change. I've been a daughter caring for aging parents, a mom navigating the shifting needs of a blended family, and a woman rediscovering herself after divorce. During those times, nature was not just a place to escape—it became my mirror, my teacher, and my sanctuary.

What I've come to believe—and now teach—is this: **We are not separate from nature. We *are* nature.**

Just like trees drop their leaves, rivers shift course, or tides rise and fall, we too move through cycles of becoming, resting, grieving, and renewing. When we reconnect with those rhythms, something inside us heals. We feel more grounded, more resilient, and more ourselves.

That's the heart of my work through **Inner-NATURALIST**: helping people reconnect to their own nature, using the outer world as a gentle guide. Whether it's a 17-minute pause under a tree, a seasonal journaling practice, or a once-in-a-lifetime retreat into the wild, every step into nature brings us closer to our truth.

To support that journey, I offer tools like:
- Sit spots and sensory awareness
- Seasonal reflection practices
- Guided nature walks and storytelling
- Neurographic drawing to unlock subconscious insight

Each tool is grounded in the cycle of the seasons—because when we stop pushing ourselves to bloom during winter, and instead learn to honor each season for what it brings, we begin to live more peacefully, more powerfully, and more in tune with our natural selves.

So wherever you are right now—feeling stuck, seeking something more, or simply curious—know this: You are welcome here.

Let's walk this path together and rediscover what it means to live in harmony with nature's wisdom—and your own. Let's grow together.

Happy Nature Connecting!

—Lari Jo

Made in the USA
Coppell, TX
16 January 2026

67486889R00059